# The Turning

**Other Books by Joanne Fedler**

*Ideological Virgins and Other Myths*
*The Knot List*
*The Dreamcloth*
*Secret Mothers' Business*
*Things Without A Name*
*When Hungry, Eat*
*The Reunion*
*It Doesn't Have To Be So Hard*
*Love in the Time of Contempt*
*Your Story: how to write it so others will want to read it*

# JOANNE FEDLER

# The Turning

## Poems from my life
### on my 50th birthday

Joanne Fedler
Write Your Story

Copyright © 2017 by Joanne Fedler

First published by Joanne Fedler Media 2017

www.joannefedler.com (publisher's website)

www.marketingmentor.live (design by Nailia Minnebaeva)

National Library of Australia Cataloguing-in-Publication data:

ISBN: 978-0-9954063-2-2

*For Bobba Chaya*
*in sacred memory of your broken heart*
*and the path you lit*
*in mine*

*Sometimes you hear a voice through the door calling you,*
*As a fish out of water hears the waves…*
*Come back. Come back.*
*This turning toward what you deeply love, saves you.*

**Rumi**

# PRELUDE TO THE POEMS

For a neurotic hypochondriac who has spent way too much time imagining 'dying young,' turning 50 is a hell of a triumph. I can officially exhale. No chance of an early departure. I cannot tell you what a relief it is.

I wanted to face this majestic anniversary with every part of me intact, to offer a full embrace of everything I am into the arms of this birthday.

What could qualify as a fitting acknowledgement of the heft and seniority of this occasion? It feels like an achievement. A summit of sorts. Not that I have any intention of heading downhill from here.

I've spent a good number of the 18 250 odd days of my existence writing. I started when I was six. I penned mawkish poetry in my teens. There I began to explore the tendrils of an inner life. It was a place I grew to trust, a refuge from heartache, fear and sorrow. I began to know myself in this fertile solitude.

My first book was published in my early thirties. Though I've now written and published ten books, I still read and write poetry as a way of tending to my own heart.

My paternal grandmother Bobba Chaya was a Yiddish poet who died in her early fifties long before I met her. In this year of my turning 50, I have felt her presence. It may be perimenopausal fancies, but I tend to believe in the soul and its gentle correspondence with the mystery. With her as a tender muse, I began to collate some of my writing.

*The Turning* is a collection of fifty poems from my life.

Many of them catch small moments of transformation, as an ending slipped into a new beginning, a choice ruptured the past or a realisation burst an illusion, awakening me a little more. Some touch on transitions, gateways, moments of leave-taking, sometimes from a self I was abandoning. Motherhood, solitude, writing and death are themes that recur, all of which have stretched me into the deep questions I have about what it means to be a person.

This book is my way of turning and bowing to everything I have experienced, with astonishment and gratitude, and to tell the days, the people and the places I have known, I deeply love them. This love, in Rumi's words has saved me.

*Joanne Fedler*
*31 August 2017*

# The Poems

# The first words of Genesis

I remember the rhythm
as we counted seconds
through the narrow
tunnel of those holy hours
not knowing
where they led

I remember the relief
of breaking waters
the white sheets wet

the midwife squeezed my hand
'*It won't be much longer now...*'

But as the night wore on
I became afraid
of what I suddenly
did not understand

'*...still only three centimeters...*'

I needed silence
no touching
not even like that
to retch alone
parched beyond thirst

a reaction to the epidural
I swore I'd never have
all ritual forsaken

'*...I think we better call the doctor...*'

When finally, I wept
'I can't...'
they wheeled me
and shaved me

and burst me
and hauled a body from my own
in one slick swipe.

*'You won't believe what I'm seeing…'*
he shuddered,
the camera unsteady in his hand:

Dawn
7.17 for the record.

All but forgotten,
I howled
into the cry of
that morning,
*What is it?*

The first words of
Genesis:
Agirlagirlagirlagirl

# Yeoville, first night

That first night
in Yeoville
I lay in my king size bed
and called the ceiling, mine
the walls, 'dearly beloved,'
the noise of motorbikes
and alchohol from the street below,
'friend.'

I knew then
that aloneness
was the key
to becoming;
how everything
had been a delay,
a long wait
to begin – this – this
quiet curiosity;

that in my own space
I'd soften
open the folds
I'd tucked tightly in,
find 'her,' that
unaccompanied girl
a stowaway til now.

I pulled back the curtains
to let the moon in,
leaned on the night's shoulder
and I told the truth
for the first time.

# The Boy and a Fork

When a mother dies young,
her offspring are quickly
dispersed
no time for trawling
the treasures she may
have left behind.
A fork is all she left
on which to perch
his heart
and all the questions
her going brought with it.
He carried that fork with him
for twenty-three years
a three-pronged pedestal
in memory of
the touch of her lips.

At the age of thirty-three
he swam out into the mist
where the sea got dark
the tears of his ancestors
touched his skin
peeling the lostness
from his grasp.

He threw that fork
into the belly of the sea;
when he swam back to shore
he was, for the first time,
all alone inside himself
the burden of that steel
now the ocean's
and what he never had
gently sank
as he strode
across the sand
marking the earth
with his freedom.

# Numinous

The Chinese say
A sheep should never marry an ox.
Still, you brought me things
like this:

*It means marked by a sense
of the presence of God.*

How else but through you
could I learn such a word?

*Like breathtaking architecture
perhaps in the landscape of a third Temple.*

I held it like a hallowed
stone
tight in the paw
of my heart

If only words could bless
and bestow,
anoint their utterers
with 'here you go…' and
'how does that feel?'

I longed
too long
for us to be marked
in the way of that word.

In the end
places were all that remained

Especially that sunny patch
in the forest
where the pine needles
were soft on my back.

# Right Turn

I chose *bona fides*
and other Latin terms you find
in law books
for it was easier, they claimed
to fall back on
precedent and *stare decisis*
than a line Tennyson wrote
that's etched in your soul.

I turned left at logic
not right at longing;
opted for laboratories
over labyrinths
became encased in cases
tried to stifle stories
heed the judgements
of reasonable men
with careful opinions
and supportive wives.

But my shadow withered
grew taut in torts
without the cry
of darkened hearts
and birds that do not sing.

In law there was no name
for the quiet snuffing
that numbed my core –
not even in Latin.

The poets called it
'the divided self'
it was all there
in The Hollow Men –
'The horror! The horror!'

I did not want to be Ophelia
even in a robe and wig
there was no honour
in being called 'your honour'
when the mirror
crack'd from side to side
and I wished that I
were dead.

And so
I freed my anchor
turned my ship
cargo-ed with
all that is born only to die

and found my way back
by the stars and their light
and the sound of the song
in the books
I would write.

# Morning Lesson

There is a hole in her grey school stockings
I note,
as she slides the tongue of her buckle strap
under and over.
'See I can do it myself,' she says.

*'Are you my mother?'* lies
on the crayoned worn coffee-table –
(only 'know' and 'could'
gave a moment's pause)
read from cover to cover
between tooth-brushing and
time to leave for school.

I check my bag for phone, glasses
when she speaks directly:
'I will never leave you.'

'What?'

'I will always be by your side.'

I pause. Swallow.
Have I been present enough for her?
Is she afraid I will die?
What can I say
to answer this gift of love
with a fitting hold?

'I'm waiting…' she says,
all bagged up and ready at the door.

'Let's go…' I stammer.
I put my hand out to hold hers,
but she bounds ahead of me
into the morning
unburdened,
free for the saying.

# Bella's Puppies

Her dog Bella
had a litter of chocolate brown
and ink black puppies
eight handfuls of blind warm flesh
squeaking and squirming in the corner
of the laundry
where she also washes the medical tubes and
disposes of her daughter's colostomy bags.
'It's like having eight newborns,' she smiles
exhaustion, her way of life
for the past ten years.
I watch her tenderly wash each pup
in a tub of warm water,
her fingers stained with the purple
of the colour she's just
applied to my hair.
She coos to them
wraps them in soft towels
lays them down side by side
like a row of buns she's just baked
she pats Bella
'Clever girl, wonderful mother,'
and turns to me, her eyes bright,
'Isn't nature wonderful?'

# Looking for Emily

At nineteen I went to the moors
I found my way to Haworth
I stayed on the third story of a BnB
with a sweet old English couple
who had a Collie dog
named Bess

I set off one morning
for High Withens
with nothing but a
camera and a journal

to walk
where Emily walked
to touch the earth
that shaped her Heathcliff
and Cathy

I found nothing
in those ruins –
a shrunken dilapidation
not the relics of the grand manor
I'd spent years imagining.

The moors are no place
to get lost
desert-like
it is easy to mistake here
for there
north for east

This I discovered
when I, cold and weary
chanced upon
a man and his dog.
I'd walked
into the next county

and with the afternoon
closing around us
I needed to walk fast
to beat the shadows
'*You don't want to*
*be stuck out here, now do you, love?*'

I ran to chase the sun
the mud clung to my boots
I had no water
my knee ached
I wanted to be
safe from
the gathering dark
and the bleak
reach of that heath.

I almost cried
when I spied a family
up ahead.

That night
I soaked in a hot bath
spooked and spent
I left early the next morning
my curiosity cured
further from Emily
and closer to myself
than I had ever been.

# Not the Bride

The photo arrives
with the noon post
amongst bills and K-mart leaflets
in front of – not behind
the 'thank you for the wonderful gift' note
in her sincere handwriting.
Your handsome smile
short-cropped hair- the way I like it –
are painfully familiar –
'this is how this relationship looks to me' you said,
turning the mirror to my face
'and this is how it looks to you', turning it to yours,
yes I smiled, 'a two-headed love.'
In the hammock of our arms
we promised our passion
would outlast hours and dust.

Now those fingers
that once played lute music
with my breasts
clutch the arm
of your gorgeous bride
as if that is all they ever knew.

She snuggles beside you
the table is strewn with rose petals – the blended kind
that make me weak with their beauty –
I hold this picture
not even trying not to weep.

You made it.
You did it.
You got there – married and finished –
without me.

How could you?
God bless you.

Is there space
in that picture
for the memory
that someone else loved you first?

Not the Bride.

# The Cats I Would Not Take Back

I brought home kittens –
they were giving them away
and who could resist?
'Take them back before you get attached,'
my father's voice a stern admonition,
'They're not staying.'

'Just wait and see them first.'

And that decided it.

I named the tabby Mystery
a mix of Miss and misty,
the ginger one
after King Alobar
from *Jitterbug Perfume*
who loved Kudra with the big nose.

Alobar became the king of the house
the lion of my father's heart
he lay beside him
in his troubled times
the soft fleece
of a kindred spirit
on the scar
across his abdomen.

He drowned in the pool
in his old age,
afloat on his saffron fur
carried to sleep on chlorine.

To lose a friend
is a mighty grief.
Yet how sweet to have known
such great love
to have been touched
in fluff and purrs
by an angel.

# What is Worth Keeping?

I take out that avocado green
dress with the beaded pearls I sewed
beneath the bust
the one you borrowed
for my wedding
it is tearing, as ageing chiffon does

I sniff it

any perfume you wore
that day has long
evaporated as smells do

as apparently people do

this dress is
a clear throwaway
but there you are
in my dress
because you had nothing to wear

caught on camera
sobbing at our vows

I do not want to be sentimental
keeping this dress
will not let me keep you

but if I can throw this out
what in this world is worth keeping?
What is keeping for
if not for dresses
such as this?
I cut out the
the beaded pearls
and discard the dress

I am getting bolder
as I get older
but at 35, what would you

have known about that?

# The Liquorice Incident

I once got my little sister
to admit she'd stolen
some liquorice that had gone missing
from my father's bedside table

I pummelled her for hours
like an interrogator
she was littler
in awe of me
and I was so certain
it was she

I exaggerated the dangers of lying
banishment from heaven
developing a taste for lies and where that leads
being struck down by God – yes, I went so far

she put up a valiant fight
*It wasn't me it wasn't me*
but as the torture wore on
her denials withered

when finally she broke
and admitted she'd dunnit
I claimed it as a triumph
over falsehood
the saving of her soul
a testament to
my brilliant detective work.

Until later
when our older sister
confessed she'd taken the liquorice.

When we denounce
terrorism
brutality

and other acts of cruelty
we forget the liquorice incident
and the tears of innocence
our little sisters cried
and the righteous victories
we claimed in pride
in the name of truth and justice
as they shattered inside.

# I Do Not Know These Feet

Outside the bathroom
lined up military style
– he is meticulous about such things –
are four pairs of basketball shoes
'airing' or 'drying'
each the length of my forearm
clown-like to my eye,
to match his six-foot frame.

Each time I pass them
on my way to the kitchen
I pause.

I knew those feet once.

One was caught under my
right rib cage
shocking me
with a swift kick
'uh-oh,' I thought,
'a fighter.'

I knew those feet
when I first slipped them
into soft shoes
he stumbled and protested
only ever having known
the earth underfoot.

I have known dirty little feet
smelly boy feet
with toenails that needed cutting.
Broken toes twisted in beach football
toes peeking from a full length cast
after a tibial break.

But the inhabitants of this menswear,
double-the-size of my own –

I do not know these feet.

# Be The Luggage

If you have ever lost
your luggage while travelling
you will appreciate
what I'm about to say
is not frivolous
on the contrary, perhaps it smacks
keenly of God:

for I have noticed
people come and go
like luggage at an airport carousel
finally claimed by their owners

perhaps then
we too are
nothing more
than baggage

humble carriers
transporting – as we do our genes –
something precious
corseted in our souls
a flicker of self

to leave behind

tasked only with parturition

a porter offloading
our only mission
to sign off on delivery
when we find, as we must,
what we've been asked
to carry into the
terminal of this life.

# What She Taught Me

Poise and beauty
to be sensible and unsentimental
that tears are not cheap
– no man worth even one –
to slave over a hot stove
how the little girl
lives inside each woman
an artist, a romantic, an occupational therapist
turned doctor – by a father's instruction
how to bend not break
care for the sick
love a pet to its last breath
to worship but not follow recipes
how to miss your darlings
within an inch of heartbreak
and how to turn to roses –
those gentle nurses of the spirit –
to fill the heart with colour.

# I Came to Write

I arrived on Whidbey Island
to be alone
Cedar Cottage all my own
afraid of what I might not find
now that I had come to write.

I asked to be someone else
not daughter
lover
activist
sister

an apprentice to story
promised only
to words

I swallowed my days
gulped the hours
circled from
desk to
armchair to
reading nook

when my eyes burned
I walked the forest tracks
listened for owls
picked flowers
and returned spilling
with sentences

once a deer appeared
at my window
as I dozed
silent and serious
before she slipped back
between the trees

I watched a spider spin her web
afresh after the rain
and so I learned
to discard
the work of my afternoons
and find a new place to start
come morning

Mount Rainier whispered
on the skyline
then crept back into
her shroud of mist
when I looked for her again

one night I dreamed
of branches bursting from my breasts
vines reaching for the moon

by then I knew
to trust the signs

and sure enough

my heartbeat echoed

one high
one low

as the moon grew round
on Puget Sound
I plumped
dividing and dividing
splintering from the inside

like a magician's fist
everything inside me
opened
to reveal
what had been
hidden there
all along.

# The Cabdriver's Cat

*I had a cat once, when I was a boy*
*it was human, this cat*

How so? I asked.

*My grandmother complained*
*how dirty it was*
*this cat,*
*she wouldn't let it sit*
*on the bed*
*after that*
*the cat always cleaned itself*
*before it jumped up to her.*

Cats are clever, I agreed.

*And then once,*
*my mother was walking past*
*the bathroom*
*and heard a strange sound*
*can you guess what it was?*

I couldn't.

*The cat was doing its business*
*on the toilet.*

I've heard you can teach a cat
to use the toilet, I ventured.

*This cat was not taught.*
*I'm telling you,*
*it was human.*

What was its name?

*No name.*

No name?

*We only had one cat.*
*We just called it*
*Cat.*

# End of Life Order

I do not want to die in nappies
raging against those who love me
protesting my innocence from mortality
caked in fear and judgements.

Let me fly away
when we can laugh together
when the body, though frail
is still well-oiled, sexy, delicious as bodies are.
Let me die in my sleep
in my joy
in my prayers
let me die laughing
full of 'remember when's…' and
'I'll never forget's…'

Let me die sparkling
smelling of summer
in sunshine
in birdsong
after a wonderful meal
having worn my best clothes
and drunk all the wines we were saving
for a special occasion

Let me die lightly
with few possessions
I can still call my own
having said all my 'I love you's' and
'I forgive you's'

Let me die in my bed
on fresh sheets of Egyptian cotton
holding his hand
with joy in my blood
my cats by my side
with the peonies I asked for
still good for days.

# Once on a Windy Day at Clovelly Beach

They throw themselves
into the surf,
little muscles flexed against the cold
tiny nipples pursed in protest,
they screech like seagulls
hopping and dancing
in their gooseflesh.
eyeing the brawn of the sea
man-to-man
throwing words like
'bloody' and 'freezing'
at the waves
in and out
'too cold,'
'let's do it again,'
at ten, boys in boxers
too cool for budgie-smugglers
shout their worst profanities
when slapped
against the rocks
and in water swallowed not spat.

*'You getting in mum?'*

I brace the cadence of
these shifting waters
between the shoulders of concrete
and follow them in
'Head under,' he reminds me,
'or it doesn't count,'
so in it goes.

For this moment
I am part of this secret truce
of boys and brine

their bodies-bursting:
only just.

I remind them to
respect the waves,
stay close
I pull them to the safety
relieved when
the wind and the water
become too much
and they scramble
up the slippery stairs.

Once out,
they huddle in towels,
making hot chocolate
with marshmallow plans
fries with *extra* chicken salt
bartering NBA dream teams
stretching into
heroes and warriors
soldiers and athletes

as I pack the bag
and shimmer softly
back
into no-one.

# *What I Knew*

I knew back then
even in the quagmire of our hunger
for whatever it was we hurted for
in each other
as I moved through the turnstile
of your affection
that someday I would look back
on the landscape of all that had passed
and linger at your smile
beneath our graduation caps
so ridiculous, really
but not quite as ridiculous
as that intermittent bobbing
of you,
along the surface of years
as a possibility
something un-lost
awaiting me.

Every now and then
I lean back to that span of days
when you possessed me
caressed me
with indifferent need
me knowing
how far you were from my reach
but also that someday
you would return to the confines
of that small New Haven room
and remember
that girl
that time
with a fragile heart.

# *Within Kindness*

Within kindness
the story of other kindnesses live
like imaginal cells
in the cacoon

the way an acorn holds
the story of the oak
or youth
keeps the secret of
old age.

I inscribed a book
– it was a gift from a friend –
I wished the reader
'strength and courage'
as she battled
unmet longing
for a child.

They were just words
and I had many other books
still to get through.

Still
she wrote back:
'I have a friend
going through a hard time
I'd like to send her a copy too.
Please write the same message for her.'

Now, as I flick open
the second book
I let myself know
the lengths of her
desolation, month after month
the Siberia of her heartache.
I offer myself

into her story
to touch
her courage
and her kindness
with my pen.

# Sending Her Home

There is talk.
The baby must be sent home.
It is time.
This language trickles
into dinner time conversations.
It seems to be decided.

Refilwe, little Pearl,
who is only a year, maybe more
is the baby
I have longed for all my life.
I am ten when she arrives.
Violet lets me change her,
hold her to my heart,
smell and feel the velvet
of her nutty brown skin.

There is a part of me that thinks she's mine.
Violet trusts me with her.
I'm allowed to take her up to my room
where I play mommy-mommy with her.

I am in love with this baby.
She is a whisper of babies-to-come.
I rehearse singing lullabies.
I feed her.
We coo back and forth.
I learn to change a nappy.
I walk with her in my
arms til she softens like
a baby koala bear into
my chest
her eyelids
flickering
with baby dreams.

Violet sometimes lets me
into her room to watch

when she baths her.
Those chubby legs,
little threads around her ankles and arms
amber beads around her neck
unexplained
but some kind of African thing.
Her body rubbed down with
Johnson's baby oil
by Violet's strong weathered hands.

She is starting to walk.
no longer content
to be strapped all day
to her mother's warm back.

This then, is why It's Time.

I cry.
I beg, don't send her away.
My parents explain the politics to me.
with long words like
Bophuthatswana
which is where she comes from.
But I know she comes from Violet
and Violet lives in our backroom.

*She needs to go to school*
*with her kind*
*It's cruel to keep her here*
*She needs to learn her language*
*Be with her people*
*It will confuse her*
*if she stays here too long*
*It's for her own good.*

I go to Violet.
What does she think?
She shrugs.
Ag, Jo, she must go.
Why? I sob.

I want to see her cry mother tears.
I want my parents to see her pain.
They are good people.
They won't inflict suffering.
But Violet's eyes grow small.
She scolds me for my heartache.
Tells me to stop crying.
Then she turns
and goes back
to folding
the laundry.

# Bubbles on You

A mirage of glass planets
cascade
falling spheres
of rainbow tears

your gasp
as your grasp
a handful of nothing

tells me you're surprised
that your eyes
tell great big bubble lies.

# Do Not Do No Harm

Do not be
harmless
as the Buddhists teach.
There is no grit in goodness.
No pearl without sand.
No butterfly whose wings
have not been distressed.

You must break promises
to yourself and others;
do the unforgiveable;
torture those you love;
hunt the fox
and then eat
its fear-stained flesh.

All this you must do
to learn that there is nowhere to go
no-one to become unless you
turn your face
towards the threat inside you.
Not until you learn
where you are jagged
brutal
irredeemable
will you become
visible to yourself.

This is what it means
to be alive:
to know your harm
like you know the freckles
on your skin;
mottles of imperfection
as guilty of sin as
the San Andreas Fault.
Like the earth is torn;

you are torn
Like it is broken,
so are you.

To do no harm
is to
shrink from shadow
as if it weren't
in you
from you,
like the outbreath.

## big clown
## little clown

we stand striped and silly
lipsticked with huge red mouths
me a whole head littler than her
her arm around my neck
girls, dressing up in a private story
I no longer remember

above my desk that picture
reminds me we share things
beyond memory
deeper than words
in the spaces language
does not go
when we spoke
in a dialect
just our own
me, her interpreter
her, my heartfriend
put together to be
what they call 'sisters
a word for
mysterysoultogetherforever
we found ways of liking
what was inevitably love at birth

big clown
big sister
wedged in me like something –
the opposite of heartache.

# What Faith is For

When the long nights of waking to feed and settle
have seeped into long ago
and all the bedtime stories that will ever be read
have been closed and shelved
when fairies of teeth
and goblins of night terrors
have left for good
when knowing where they slept –
in that bed you made and remade –
is a privilege of the past,
you must harvest the wish from the bone,
the happily-ever-afters from every once-upon-a-time,
the dreams from every peaceful sleep
and burrow down into the nest of your chest
where not-knowing must suffice
and all you can do is trust
in unseen benevolence
to shepherd and watch over them
where your eyes cannot go
and your footsteps cannot follow.

Under other rooves, and in strange beds
and down dark alleys they go
and all you have to hold onto
is your prayer that shadows them
like the tail of a comet

*Keep them safe*
*Keep them safe*

This, this then,
is what faith is for.

# A Wedding Poem

She who is afraid of promises
of longing after girlish insubstantials
and other romantic oscillations
she who is part-gypsy: the wandering sort
never believed in twin-soul nonsense
or grand declarations of endless love
she who set out with 'one day at a time'
now finds close to a decade shared
with one who began
as a friend, nothing more.

She who wandered through the desert
sharing stories of The Promised Land
with her companion,
who offered an ear, a shoulder, a hand,
small body parts for shelter
never understood that the land she sought
was the space between the reach of his fingertips
and her own.
Until now.

She who whispered to God, 'give me Heathcliff,'
so she could be loved, wutheringly, like Cathy,
got Zed, so she could be loved sanely
evenly, perpetually,
through 34 hours of paralysed labour
through colic
and roseola
and grommets
and tantrums
through the darkest night of the soul
the shattering of faith
the crossing of oceans
the ubuntu-lessness of being here.

She who once strode in thigh-high black boots
shuffles now in slippers

stripped of all the tantalizations of youth
finds that love grows
in these quiet places
between phonecalls to say,
'Can I pick up anything on my way home?'
and shared mouthfuls of
his particular mixture
of ice cream and yoghurt
during ad breaks in Average Joe.

For all this and the dreams he paints
of two wrinkled companions
she writing, he pottering,
in their little shack by the sea
she is ready
to be wrong
about everything

to thrust herself
into this vow
like a bird
into the wide
welcoming arms
of the invisible wind.

# In The Dreaming

I dreamed of a boy
from my youth
a boy I never had
– not in any sense of the word –
though I loved him through another girl
a friend, I once imagined, around whose
shoulders his strong arms slung
and for whom his lopsided
smile was meant.

I claimed him
not in his touch
but in the ache he planted in me
for what I knew
with each cell of my body
I wanted.

Never
wishy-washy
uncertain,
lacking direction or purpose
– anything but –
I was driven
to fill that wanting.

In years to come
I wrote as if each word would make good
his arms around her shoulders
and now, ten years in the writing
my passion hovers near completion
and that boy comes to me in my dreams
embraces me
meets the eagerness of my lips
with his warm mouth
at last!
And I laugh, even in sleep
for how boys
and books
get muddled
in the dreaming.

# Housework Poems

I fold the sheets
corner to corner
the way my nanny taught me
it is easier to fold a letter
or a serviette
but not something
bigger than you:
a freshly washed sheet;
a newly sprung grief.

Dishes love a good soap
a hot tap
to rinse their faces
they prefer warm towels
to be stacked neatly
they mind how you hold them.

I walk past that cockroach carcass
maybe three dozen times
no-one else picks it up
so there it stays
between the dining room table
and the laundry door
leg severed
carnage of Jinx's midnight pranks
until we have guests coming
and I vacuum it up
lest they think
'What kind of people are they?'

The broom sweeps me up
like a broken teacup
and nudges me into a corner
where the cobwebs meet
to discuss the ant problem
and the dust affair.

Knives don't like to be contradicted
forks refuse to discuss politics
but spoons just smile
and hold out their empty hands.

The teapot pours me
into the porcelain cup
I flow easily
and let off plenty of steam.

My reading glasses
put me on
and sigh
'Ah, clear at last!'

# Boy

My oestrogen skyrockets
circles him in pinks and reds
drawing life to his
perfect five-fingered hand
long nose
deep set forehead
littlest penis
marbles of testicles
which when I see them –
shadows on a scan –
make me laugh out loud
for how I,
inflamed with oestrogen
could make those parts

his coming
to me
from me
through me
is the deepest secret yet

he courses his testosterone
through my veins
makes me magical,
yangs my yin
as I, meloned and lush,
pulse with incongruous
masculinity

I must have made him
but he has boy-ed me,
brought me to term
to show me

just what little boys
are made of.

# Dissatisfaction

I am afraid of
getting lost
in small satisfactions

rituals
that placate
routines designed
never to disrupt
or disturb.

I must live near water
it's got to do with the horizon,
you understand

calling the eye
to what lies beyond
*look, look*
*there is more*
*much more...*

Isn't that
ultimately
what dissatisfaction is?

Without this discontent,
I am not meant for dishes
garbage
laundry
or even love

I lust for
passion's impatience
underworlds
the secret life
that bubbles
and gnaws.

Like the sea,
I sigh and heave
throwing up a whale
here and there
all creation
concealed
beneath a briney
hunger.

# The Vow

When you ask the question
'To what am I vowed?'
you step through
the rubble of your life
untie your buttons
loosen your belt
your hair may shed its leaves
even your bones may melt
as you stretch yourself
like a kite into
the air
as if gravity
were a choice.

There is a family
beyond and through
the families to whom
we are indentured in mortality
a holy tribe – angels perhaps –
who shoulder us
in secret correspondence
counselling us
in dreams
and other emptinesses.

There are promises
that have come before
that hold us steady from above
though we stumble below;
oaths that tempt us to
pull back the curtain of housekeeping
and fix our eyes
on the path
further than our window
calling us elsewhere.

While we inhabit
the smoky cabin of this life

tend the soup
sweep the floors,
we can sometimes
close our eyes
and catch the call
outside our door
and beyond that,
the endless sky
calling us home.

# What The Blood Knows

I dreamed of a story
of a time and place
I never knew

tales half-spoken
and almost-lost
I breathed
and brewed.

Three tellings
I wove into a cloth of words
fragments of Yiddish
stitched to ghosts of
Naryshkin Park
and graves unmarked.

*Where did it come from?*
you ask and ask
and I, for one
do not know
to say

the wheel of lineage
turns its quiet way

I catch
a spillage of song
from a village
long lost

I feel the hand of the poet

as the seamstress sews

I know it
seems strange
to arrange the veins
to find the light

as I write with these hands
to understand
why I talk of things
that make me cry
for reasons
only the blood knows why.

# Little Pink Lines

Let us give thanks
for the Two Pink Lines
for their prophecy
their potency
their quiet seeping rendition
of change
for their humble announcement
their cataclysmic message
their humour and irony.
Let us laugh with them
at the way in which
what the body knows
the heart only learns
after a good piss.
God bless the soul
that speaks
in little pink lines.

# In The Light of this Knowing

Three times I have been
on the right side of coincidence
not the everyday kind
of thinking about so-and-so
and then bumping into them
or having a dream about a bird
only to be shat on by one the next day
trust me, I've had my fair share of those too
and I don't mind what you make of those
but I'm talking about
the shake your bones
*Are you paying attention?*
*What are the chances?* kind
that would make mathematicians
and scientists pause.

Each one has saved my life:

first came the rain
that would not stop
ten hours it poured
a broken down car
a mechanic (not a mystic)
who uttered
'Someone up there is looking
after you.'

Next a lifechanging letter
was delivered to my hands
despite my having moved twice
since the address on the envelope.

Lastly, there was jetlag
in the middle of the night
and a black gloved hand
that pulled the curtains aside
and if I hadn't been there…

well I was, and I'm here to tell
the story.

If what I am telling you is true
it cannot be
that life is random
'everything happens for a reason'
despite its schmaltziness
must hold steady.

I tell you this so that
if I ever I should succumb
to the narcissism of disbelief
fancying God as a 'nice-to-have'
notion in my back pocket
a sad fiction
for the irrational
and the intellectually crippled

you have my permission to slap me
(verbally, of course, I don't subscribe to violence)
because not only do I have
hard evidence
to the contrary

but in the light of this knowing

there is nothing left
in this world
to fear.

# Song to Myself

She who always knew
that she was destined – destined, mind you –
for more than domesticity
never suspected that perhaps her knowing
might be nothing more than the soul's delusion
holding imprints of hopeful mystery.
This knowing comes now to bother her
in the hubble and clutter of kids-cats-anniversaries
to a dissatisfaction
an impatience
with the humble goodness of her ordinary life.
As if she needed reminding that
the envelope of options
is sealed now
and the unfurling of
what will be has become a matter of
unmagical consequence.
She who longed both for this
and for a roaming otherness
now remembers past lovers
and the taste of their tongues
as she fights the shame
of a temper at small infractions by her
children-thank-god-for them
never knew such temper simmered
aching to be lost.
She sinks into memories and dreams
folding corners of herself down
like a neat napkin
hiding the stains, the dirt
of her most wondrous gypsy self
so that this life – this perfectly happy life –
might proceed without incident
medication
tragedy.
She who writes this song to herself
sings now for the selves
that have no place
to be sung.

# Always a Traveler

A woman sits down at a table
removes a journal –
paper, pen, pencil
and inhaling deeply
moves her hand
to the page.

She closes her eyes
tracking
the animal that lives
deep in her jungle

she summons it
from silence only by

wrestling words
watching
waiting

here she learns patience
for that soft creature will not
be commanded to attendance

a spotting never guaranteed

many a journey
undertaken in vain.

But then

when it finally slips
between her fingers
she looks away
so as not to frighten

overwhelm

ask too much

she keeps her hand moving,
feigning nonchalance
a paragraph,
a page, more?
before its ears prick
and it is gone.

She returns
time upon time
to chance upon
her own endangered wildlife

to glimpse
what is hidden
to know it
is not forgotten

to untame herself
from the name
by which she is known
outside her writing.

She leaves quiet tracks

words here and there

evidence of her passage

always a traveler
between two worlds

the one in which she
strains and serves
and the one
in which she saves
her life.

# Choose Your Exit

The way Leonard Cohen put it
death will come at us
like a bullet from the blue
a hit and run
a hungry wolf
we never saw coming.

But maybe he was wrong
(forgive me Leonard).
Maybe death isn't unchosen
like that wave you didn't calculate
would pull you under
or that tumour
you didn't know was there
until it was too late.

Perhaps just as we pick our parents
we pick our undoing
not consciously, of course –
(the software we're using
considers death a virus) –
but perhaps unknowingly,
curled in the umbilicus
of consciousness
like an unspoken wish
is an awoken spot
which feels with keen sorrow –
but also knows how to keep a secret –
that to be born,
we must die,
sometime in the future
when we've forgotten
the terms of our human birth
and are grandiose
with breath and blood.

There perhaps
rests this impossible thought:

that we will reach
for our chosen exit,
in one last flourish
of our perfect singularity
signing out
with a distinctive departing
signature, like the graffiti
you see on tree-trunks and
sidewalks,
I was the one who left
*by stormy fire*
*by flaming water*
*by slow decline*
*in an act of passion*
*after too much wine*
*drunk and in a fight*
*dropping from the sky*
*on the 11th day of Fall.*

# Halved

I made her need me
because I needed
to be needed
once I held her closer
than lungs
deep in my gut.

Then I made rules
about when to be needed
and how to be needed
I brought the sky
down to human scale
and said, 'that is all'
and even, 'enough.'

And now who can blame her
as she howls and rages
bashes and batters
at me with fists
not knowing
how things
become undone
and at the incongruity
of suddenly being two
when we were always
one?

# Unfollowed

No-one can live too long
in the spotlight
(actors and politicians try
– if you call that living).

In the glare
of perpetual exposure
delicate organs are
scorched

the soul was not made for
such climates
it craves foliage,
protection from inspection

we must disappear
from view
dip beneath the horizon
be lost to the world
now and then

we were also built for silence
why else
do we lose ourselves
from noise in
dreams
prayer
astonishment?

We have a face
not for profile pictures
comment
likes
or follows

to find it
we must go alone

without witnesses
fans
friends or family

we belong too
to this
Otherland.

To be unfollowed
we must follow ourselves
reach for the
plush hush
of going nowhere
pleasing no-one
promising nothing.

In this hermitage
the heart summons
its wearer back:

*'Who are you?*
*Where did you come from?*
*And why are you here?'*

# Truth and Reconciliation

Who was there for her
when your child cried out
from a nightmare?
Who explained to her
why girls must bleed
to become women
to soften her fear
that she was dying?
Did she ever ask:
Mama where were you?
And did you ever speak the truth –
that it was white children
you rocked to sleep at night?
That it was for
strangers' little ears
that you clucked sounds of
*Tula baba* comfort
and taught your songs?

You were our mother
Wooden spoon spanker
Tucker-inner
Storyteller
Maltabela-maker
Baby-sitter
Doek-wearer
Pap-sharer.

Until we learned to call you
Domestic worker
Chore-shirker
Shebeen-queen
Of pap-n-gravy cuisine
with a standard eight
and steel mugs you can't break
Backroom boarder
Old-clothes hoarder

for your people back home
who phone
to tell you
your daughter passed away
the day before yesterday
AIDS-related complications
no further explanations.

Who was there for her
when she cried out
from pain?
Who explained to her
why boys must wear condoms
to stop girls
from infection?
Did she ever ask:
Mama, where are you?
before she slipped
away?

How did you stay
another day?
How did you hold onto
your heart's estrangement
as you made
your own child's
funeral arrangements?

You were *her* mother
No other
Clicked your tongue
Buried your young
Covering with earth
The child you birthed.

There can be no reconciliation
or compensation
for this desecration
of your appointed designation

Forced into surrogacy
to mother the ungracious
instead of your own
to whom
you and your songs
only ever
rightfully
belonged.

# Laid Bare

Mothering was upon me
a migraine of effort
and
suddenly it left
lifted and peeled
a miracle cure.

A cure for what?

Newly naked
uncaked
no more treatment required
'You're free to get on with your life...'
I am bewilderingly healed
bereft
shorn and unsure
re-formed
still feeling blindly
for the shape
of this self

clean and whole
like a newly laid
egg.

# It Never Goes Away

It is the most
treacherous of ideas
that people do not go away
though bodies do
(how can they?)

And yet
it is
the only answer
now that you have ventured into
that dark sky
out of turn
you, bug-eyed
laugh-riddled
amber curled
all girl
gone one day
severed from this sunshine
shorn from new mornings
without warning.

Did you arrive someplace
dear friend
in the way going
implies a coming
even in the absence of witnesses?
Did God come down and
take your hand?

Did you meet
the unborn pea
inside you,
like a mother's homecoming?

It never goes away

this longing to know
that you did not end.

# Love Affair

He bought me a new computer,
but did not understand why
I had to have the
luminous
pink
keyboard
that cost extra.

'The keys feel bouncier,'
and 'it's pretty.'

*'What's wrong with the keyboard
that comes with the computer?'*

It was grey for starters.

He shrugged
shook his head,
the way he does when he thinks
I'm being careless with money.

But never mind.

You have to lay your fingers down
feel your hands on its body
press your stories into its squares,
whisper your words into its
alphabet ears.

It's a love affair
a two-way business
between a writer and
her pink keyboard
that calls her,
*come write,*
*don't go yet,*
*touch me,*
*let's run away together.*

# Unlikely Saviour

It started
in an unlikely encounter
on the Durban beachfront
after he came back early
from one of his easy lays,
and suggested a walk
on the promenade.

The night sky
leaned in as
we spoke in that fraught
deeply subtexted way
of two people
igniting a fuse
between them.

Then – like in the movies –
the rain came

we ran for cover

under shelter
he hauled me
by his strong arms
like a net full of fish
into the boat of his chest
and he kissed me
his lips warm
our faces wet,
my heart thundering
like a stampede of wildebeest,
rupturing the line
between me and men forever,
marking me with
unsugared, unspiced
Desire.

He steered me out

to where it was dark and deep
and I could no longer see
where I'd come from,
and on that ocean,
I threw off
the anchor
that stretched all the way
to the gas chambers
or the destruction of the First Temple,
or whenever it is Jews decide
our special genocide
make us Slaves to Our Suffering.
No longer
bitch to my birthright;
I broke the sacred covenant of
to only touch circumcised cock.

The sex led to love
or something close to it.
Enough for him to promise:
'If anyone ever lays a finger on you
I'll beat the shit out of him.'

I rowed my way
out of my childhood,
on a foreskinned boat,
with my first love –
who betrayed me –
but who also saved me
in that unlikely
way of a rough tough
gentle soul
who stood like Moses
with the Egyptians
bearing down
and parted that sea
so I could walk clean through it
and into a woman
no-one would
ever hit again.

# Under The Angels

Alone I am someone else
even my closest ones would find strange
in the company of cats and lanterns
I sit in this room under the angels
on the ceiling
and gather my questions:

*Who am I when I'm*
*wanting things I don't want?*

*All the stuff, I've kept – why?*

*What is still sacred when*
*we've broken the basics?*

*Was this what I wanted?*

*Could I have wanted other things?*

*What happened to that gold bracelet?*

*Has everything already been said?*

*What is calling me through the years?*

*Who fought for me other than me?*

*Shouldn't have had the cheese.*

*To know God, that's all –*

*Why is it so hard?*

The screaming tentacles of life
murderous mortgage
hungry phone
quicksand of email
all the opinions – enough!

Oh to fall out
of the poisoning world
find soft time
quiet light
trust only the vegetables
rest in the brew of family
have faith in the kids
safely in their own lives.

Let me find one precious thing to call 'here'
like this voice that comes through me
when I am alone
under the angels.
Sink only into this heaven
this peace.

# Wisdom

The guru got drunk

The shaman was shmarmy

The priest was a pedophile

The rabbi, a rogue

The maven was a maniac

The doctor was dirty

The poet was a poser

The expert was dull

The mentor was manic

The specialist didn't listen

The professor was lecherous

The healer was a hedonist

The minister, a narcissist

The doyen, a douchebag

The idol, a creep

The princess, a bitch

The Rockstar a sybarite.


But the sunrise didn't lie
or try to sell me anything.

# The Birth of Your Story

Avid reader
book lover
writer at heart
had your family
or let that ship pass by
called 'smart' from the start
rescued and raised others
done your duty
left when you needed to
stayed too long
in 'maybe' and 'someday.'
One breast less
three kids gone
hubby at the footy
with his new wife
or tombstoned too soon.
Hubby? You always did prefer girls
– not in *that* way, but mind you…
Said enough goodbyes
to a uterus
a pregnancy
a mother
(don't get you started on
friends losing fights to this and that).
A woman of letters
you always loved words.
Something there, you thought
but there was no rent in writing
and what would you write about?
– such an unremarkable life of sacrifice –
and who would care?
Read some good books lately
wanted to travel
thought you would someday
dreamed of more
but not 'stuff '– you're done with all that.
Pants getting tighter

– that's what happens over forty –
your heart's feeling lighter
you linger a little longer
in 'maybe it's not too late.'

You put on what you've put off
spent what you've been saving
for that rainy day
because
it's time
and you can
and the wait for
whatever it was you were hoping for
is done.
As words come to you
you let yourself wonder
'Maybe it's time...'
All that was lost
returns to be found.
You are not too late.
Your story is waiting
for you.

# Not Under My Roof

The way to look at this
is that there will be fewer dishes to wash
less waiting time to use the only
bathroom she can take her sweet time in,
less mess, for certain
no more scrambled egg bits
left in the sink for me clean.

The way to approach this
is with gladness
of a job well done
for what else
could any mother wish
but that she
is no longer needed
in *that* way?

Yes, I believe in wings –
I am a great proponent of nest-fleeing –
especially as an idea,
and as it relates to one's
own leave-taking,
but it is more rakish
in practice,
by which I mean
it is equally a robust grief
as it is a relief
when it is your roof
under which
she will no longer
come home to sleep.

As for me
I shuffle between these
mischievous heart-turns
where I am
at once sweet with

'*fly, my love, fly free,*'
and silly
oh so ludicrous
with *who now will I be?*

# Drowning

You will drown in air, eventually.
There will come the hour when
you will exhale for the last time
and leave breathing behind.
You once believed
this betrayal by oxygen
was the tragedy of being
earthed to flesh,
mortgaged to bones.
Every moment you love
will leave you
widowed to your history
and closer to your sinking.

You will spend half your life
with your back to the edge of this knowledge
as you find ways to lose yourself
in mirrors and malls
and aimless collections
of somnolent objects
that even you know,
will not travel.

Yet that will not stop you from
having laser-treatment on your bikini line
getting those $450 shoes you will wear twice
sending lawyers letters about that leak
which will never go away
gaining weight
losing sleep
over a constellation of
consuming consternations
that will chew up
your vitality
like a hungry ghost.

Then, somewhere in the middle
of your life,

your retina will crack
– or so it will seem –
dislodging your vision
and you will finally see
you've been looking
up the arse of your life
all along,
thinking it was a view.

Everything will shrink
til you can hold what matters
in the palm of your hand:
                the way the cat, being stroked,
winks at you with her skinny eyes
til by an act of feline ventriloquism
her purr comes from your own throat;

                on the beach on that pregnant morning
that humpback whale
whisking itself into the air
to taste the wind,
you, its sole witness;

                creeping under his chin, into his chest
and whispering *thanks for him*
against his closed eyelids
into a third silent presence;

                that night, around the campfire
hearing for the first time your daughter's voice
singing into the tree's ears
'… the lovers, the dreamers and me…'

All that remains
are those uninflected instants when
you had to remind yourself
to inhale
– not because you'd forgotten how –
but because you'd reached some kind of
fullness

another drop
and your ventricles might burst.

But you sucked oxygen
like a newborn,
you awoke back into time
your alveoli humming
your bones moist,
knowing that when the moment comes
you will surrender that last breath
like a purr,
a leap,
a prayer,
a song

and drown in
love.

# Acknowledgements

I am grateful to these poets who have sanctified my life with their words:

*Rumi*
*Hafiz*
*Kahlil Gibran*
*Rainer Maria Rilke*
*Nazim Hikmet*
*W B Yeats*
*Tennyson*
*T S Eliot*
*Theodor Seuss Geisel*
*William Stafford*
*Shel Silverstein*
*Pablo Neruda*
*John O Donohue*
*Yehuda Amichai*
*Dylan Thomas*
*Phillip Larkin*
*e e cummings*
*Robert Frost*
*Wendell Berry*
*Maya Angelou*
*Billy Collins*
*Mary Oliver*
*David Whyte*
*Bob Dylan*
*Naomi Shihab Nye*
*Leonard Cohen*
*Galway Kinnell*

and innumerable others who have helped me burrow into the deep tissue of my soul.

My beloved friend Ilze and I feed each other poetry across oceans. This collection is largely a testament to our shared love which runs like a golden thread across time, a language we speak to each other through separation. When I thought of one person who might read this book, her dear face and delight kept me on task.

I am grateful to the dazzlingly creative Nailia Minnebaeva who designed this book so that when I first saw the cover, it took my breath away. I am awed by her commitment to beauty in everything she touches.

I thank Norie Libradilla, my wonderful assistant who has been a silent heart of support in this process.

Thanks too to Karen McDermott of Serenity Press who guided me and my team with generosity to Joanne Fedler Media's first publication.

Finally I want to acknowledge all those who have inspired me to write these poems – my children, husband, cats, lovers, family, friends, strangers, Emily Bronte, Hedgebrook Writers' Colony and my darling friend Emma with whom I'd love to have celebrated my 50th birthday if she hadn't left so soon.

Joanne Fedler is an internationally bestselling author of ten books including *The Dreamcloth*, *Secret Mothers' Business* and *When Hungry, Eat*. She is a writing mentor and inspirational speaker. Before she became an author, she worked as a women's rights activist in the anti-violence against women movement in South Africa where she set up and ran a not-for-profit organization for many years.

Her first novel *The Dreamcloth* was shortlisted for the Commonwealth Prize for Fiction. Since then, her books have sold over 650 000 copies worldwide, and two have been #1 Amazon bestsellers.

In 2015 she launched her WINGS programme (Words Inspire, Nourish and Grow the Spirit) which encompasses free 7 day writing challenges, the transformational Author Awakening Adventure online writing course and soon, a writing competition.

For the past six years, she's been taking groups of aspiring women authors on writing retreats (to Fiji, Bali and Tuscany) to help them find their voices. Alumnae of her retreats and writing courses are invited to become part of her Author Liftoff programme where she nurtures aspiring authors towards publication.

Her latest book *Your Story: how to write it so others will want to read it* was published by Hay House in July 2017.

www.joannefedler.com
www.authorawakening.com
www.joannefedler.com/your-story

Lightning Source UK Ltd.
Milton Keynes UK
UKHW040717191121
394250UK00002B/317